Homonyms Synonyms & Antonyms Activity Book

By
Karen Shackelford

A Reading FUNdamentals™ Book

Other books in this series include:

Compound Words Activity Book
Nouns Activity Book
Verbs & Adverbs Activity Book
Adjectives Activity Book
Collective Nouns Activity Book
Prefixes & Suffixes Activity Book
Idioms Activity Book
Similes Activity Book

Chart Sets in this series include:

Homonyms, Synonyms & Antonyms Chart Set
Compound Words Chart Set
Nouns Chart Set
Verbs & Adverbs Chart Set
Adjectives Chart Set
Collective Nouns Chart Set
Prefixes & Suffixes Chart Set
Idioms Chart Set
Similes Chart Set

All of the titles in our
Reading FUNdamentals™ series
are also available as E-Books.

Visit us at www.barkercreek.com
for more information.

BARKER CREEK

Homonyms, Synonyms & Antonyms

Book Author: Karen Shackelford
Illustrator: Terri Oberg
Graphic Designer: Vickie Spurgin

Printed in the USA

ISBN: 978-1-928961-11-6
Item Number: LL-1600

BARKER CREEK

P.O. Box 2610
Poulsbo, WA 98730
www.barkercreek.com
800.692.5833

D0992809

Note from the Author

Basic skills are so important in the reading and writing process. **Reading comprehension** and **fluency** are enhanced when children know the various parts of speech. They also become better communicators when given these important "tools". Learning about verbs, nouns, and such doesn't seem too exciting, but when presented in a FUN way, students can enjoy participating in the learning process.

It was not my goal to write an entire book series, I simply wanted to help my own children learn some of the basic language arts skills they seemed to be missing. As I began developing a few lessons, I noticed that my children (third grade and fifth grade) were actually enjoying the activities and were LEARNING!

It then became my goal to provide both teachers and parents with the "tools" they could use to help teach and reinforce the BASICS.

The books are simple in format and easy to use. Each book in the Reading FUNdamentals™ series focuses on ONE MAIN SKILL with other skills integrated throughout the lessons. Clever illustrations are provided to help visual learners. Loaded with FUN activities, each book is designed to add more "tools" to the student's learning toolbox of basic skills.

Enjoy!

Karen Shackelford

Karen Shackelford

About the Author
Karen Shackelford is a former classroom teacher. Several of her books have been awarded with the coveted Teacher's Choice Award.

About the Illustrator
Terri Oberg is an art teacher in the Fort Worth ISD in Fort Worth, Texas.

THANKS to my creative team!
Shelly Dreiling, Terri Oberg, Gayla Sellers, Susan Munguia (story/poetry writer), and Vickie Spurgin (graphic designer)

TABLE OF CONTENTS

How to Use This Book

Please read this entire page before getting started.

There are three main sections in this book; **homonyms**, **synonyms**, and **antonyms**. Within each section, there are 11 related lessons, all in a similar format. You may choose to use these lessons as an INTRODUCTION of the skill or simply for a REVIEW of the skill.

Page Set Up

1. Set it in concrete!
Say the word, write the word neatly, then spell it WITHOUT looking at the word. Look at the word to check your spelling.

2. Nail it down!
Use the dictionary to define the word.

3. Create a blueprint!
Draw the word.

4. Tack it on!
You may need to use a separate piece of paper for some of these activities. Many are "hands-on" extensions. These can be done in a whole group setting, individually or for homework.

5. Dig in!
Write a sentence using the correct meaning(s) for each word(s).

Review Test

Measure what your students have learned. See the test on page 39.

Answer Key

HOMONYM	SYNONYM	ANTONYM
1. week	1. pail - bucket	1. adult
2. right	2. luggage - suitcase	2. melted
3. mail	3. doctor - physician	3. miniature
4. tail	4. rig - truck	4. near
5. knight	5. cook - chef	5. finish
	6. fuel - gas	6. frozen
	7. bug - insect	7. summer

Blank Page Templates

Templates for each type of word (*homonym, synonym,* and *antonym*) are provided on pages 40-42. Use these templates to create activity pages for words of your choice.

Picture Cards

There are 55 related REPRODUCIBLE pictures on pages 43-48 to supplement the lessons.

Here are some ideas for using the pictures:

- **Flash cards**
  After every lesson, give each student the related picture to color and glue onto an index card. Keep in library pockets or small bags for flash card games.

- **Riddles**
  Have the students make up riddles and allow the class to answer the riddles by holding up the correct picture card.

- **Creative Stories**
  Provide students with five to ten various pictures to incorporate in a creative writing lesson. The story could be in rebus form where pictures are used in place of words.

- **Alphabetical order**
  Put the pictures in ABC order.

- **Mini books**
  Put the picture cards in a book format to take home and enjoy.

- **Go Fish!**
  Make **four** of the *homonyms,* *synonyms* and *antonyms* pictures. Using cardstock, print four copies of the homonyms pictures. Cut into individual cards and store in a library pocket or small bag when not in use. Repeat with the synonyms and antonyms pictures to create additional GO FISH games. Great for a center activity!

HOMONYMS

What is a homonym?

A word that sounds the same as another word but has a different spelling and meaning.

WORD LIST

- flour/flower
- bare/bear
- male/mail
- sale/sail
- night/knight
- hare/hair
- week/weak
- blue/blew
- write/right
- tail/tale
- fair/fare

Reading FUNdamentals™
HOMONYMS

Name: _____

flour • flower

Set in concrete!

Say it! Write it! Spell it!

Say it!	Write it!	Spell it! (Don't look!)
flour		
flower		

Nail it down!

Define it!

What does it mean? Look it up in the dictionary.

flour _____

_____

flower _____

_____

Create a blueprint!

Draw it!

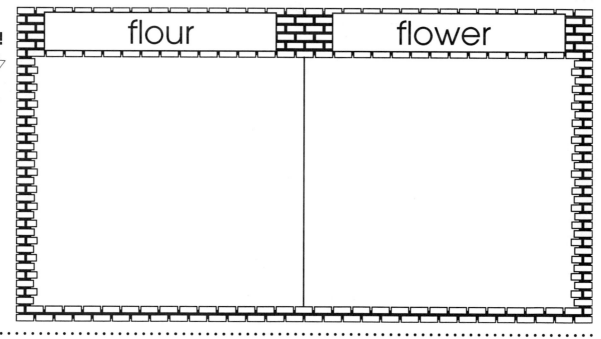

flour	flower

Tack it on!

Extend it!

Make sugar cookies from scratch. Using cookie cutters, cut them into flower shapes. Bake, decorate, and enjoy. YUM! YUM!

Dig in!

Use it!

Write each word in a sentence.

1. **flour**: _____

2. **flower**: _____

 Reading FUNdamentals™ — Homonyms, Synonyms & Antonyms ©2009 Barker Creek Publishing, Inc. • www.barkercreek.com

Name: _____

bare • bear

Set in concrete!

Say it! Write it!
Spell it!

	Say it!	Write it!	Spell it! (Don't look!)
	bare		
	bear		

Nail it down!

Define it!

What does it mean? Look it up in the dictionary.

bare _____

_____

bear _____

_____

Create a blueprint!

Draw it!

bare	bear

Tack it on!

Extend it!

On a large piece of paper, create a barefoot bear. Paint the bottoms of your feet and place them on the paper (heels together and feet separated about three inches). Let dry. The toes serve as ears. Add the face, eyes, nose and mouth using markers.

Dig in!

Use it!

Write each word in a sentence.

1. **bare:** _____

2. **bear:** _____

male • mail

Set in concrete!

Say it! Write it! Spell it!

Say it!	Write it!	Spell it! (Don't look!)
male		
mail		

Nail it down!

Define it!

What does it mean? Look it up in the dictionary.

male _____

_____

mail _____

_____

Create a blueprint!

Draw it!

male	mail

Tack it on!

Extend it!

Write a short letter to a male member of your family. This could be your dad, brother, grandpa, uncle or cousin. Place the letter in an envelope, address, and send. Be sure to add a stamp!

Dig in!

Use it!

Write each word in a sentence.

1. **male**: _____

2. **mail**: _____

Name: _____

sale • sail

Set in concrete!

Say it! Write it! Spell it!

Say it!	Write it!	Spell it! (Don't look!)
sale		
sail		

Nail it down!

Define it!

What does it mean? Look it up in the dictionary.

sale _____

_____

sail _____

_____

Create a blueprint!

Draw it!

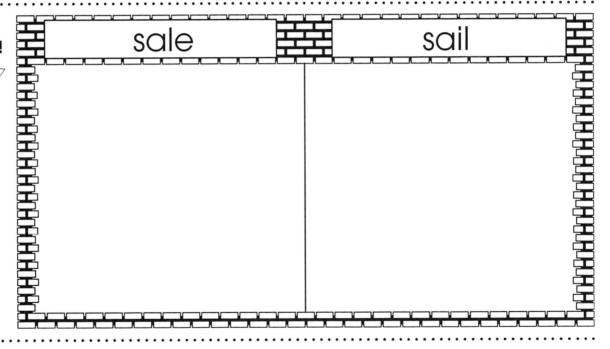

sale | sail

Tack it on!

Extend it!

Design a small sailboat using various scrap items such as fabric, straws, plastic tubs, etc. Next, write an advertisement for the newspaper with the caption, "**Check out this sailboat! It's on SALE!**"

Dig in!

Use it!

Write each word in a sentence.

1. **sale**: _____

2. **sail**: _____

Name: _____

night • knight

Set in concrete!

Say it! Write it! Spell it!

Say it!	Write it!	Spell it! (Don't look!)
night		
knight		

Nail it down!

Define it!

What does it mean? Look it up in the dictionary.

night _____

_____

knight _____

_____

Create a blueprint!

Draw it!

night	knight

Tack it on!

Extend it!

Write a short story containing three to five paragraphs about a knight who does funny things at night. Be creative!

Dig in!

Use it!

Write each word in a sentence.

1. **night**: _____

2. **knight**: _____

Name: _____

hare • hair

Set in concrete!

Say it! Write it! Spell it!

	Say it!	Write it!	Spell it! (Don't look!)
	hare		
	hair		

Nail it down!

Define it!

What does it mean? Look it up in the dictionary.

hare _____

_____

hair _____

_____

Create a blueprint!

Draw it!

hare	hair

Tack it on!

Extend it!

Look through some magazines and find a picture of a person. Cut out his or her hair. Glue this "wig" onto a separate piece of paper and add a hare's face and body. Do not forget his long, floppy ears!

Dig in!

Use it!

Write each word in a sentence.

1. **hare**: _____

2. **hair**: _____

Name: _____

week • weak

Set in concrete!

Say it! Write it! Spell it!

Say it!	Write it!	Spell it! (Don't look!)
week		
weak		

Nail it down!

Define it!

What does it mean? Look it up in the dictionary.

week _____

_____

weak _____

_____

Create a blueprint!

Draw it!

week	weak

Tack it on!

Extend it!

On a separate piece of paper, list the days of the week. Next to each day, write five VERBS describing activities that you could DO that day. Be sure each verb begins with the beginning letter for that particular day of the week. (Example: Monday-march) After this week, you will not be weak, you will be strong!

Dig in!

Use it!

Write each word in a sentence.

1. **week:** _____

2. **weak:** _____

Name: _____

blue • blew

Reading FUNdamentals™
HOMONYMS

Set in concrete!

Say it! Write it! Spell it!

Say it!	Write it!	Spell it! (Don't look!)
blue		
blew		

Nail it down!

Define it!

What does it mean? Look it up in the dictionary.

blue _____

_____

blew _____

_____

Create a blueprint!

Draw it!

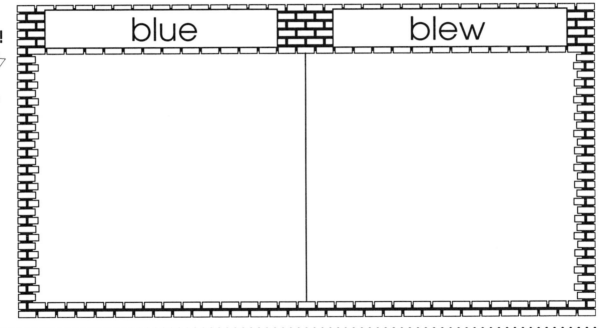

| blue | blew |

Tack it on!

Extend it!

Illustrate this sentence: **The blue kite blew in the wind.**

Dig in!

Use it!

Write each word in a sentence.

1. **blue**: _____

2. **blew**: _____

Name: _____

write • right

Set in concrete!

Say it! Write it! Spell it!

Say it!	Write it!	Spell it! (Don't look!)
write		
right		

Nail it down!

Define it!

What does it mean? Look it up in the dictionary.

write _____

_____

right _____

_____

Create a blueprint!

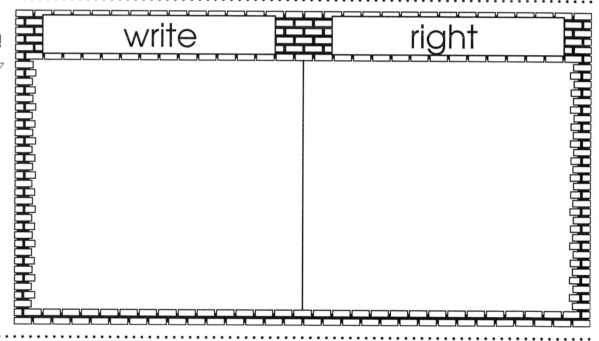

Draw it!

write	right

Tack it on!

Extend it!

Try to write your name using *your toes* on your *right foot*. Good luck!

Dig in!

Use it!

Write each word in a sentence.

1. **write:** _____

2. **right:** _____

Name: _____

tail • tale

Reading FUNdamentals™
HOMONYMS

Set in concrete!

Say it! Write it!
Spell it!

Say it!	Write it!	Spell it! (Don't look!)
tail		
tale		

Nail it down!

Define it!

What does it mean? Look it up in the dictionary.

tail _____

_____

tale _____

_____

Create a blueprint!

Draw it!

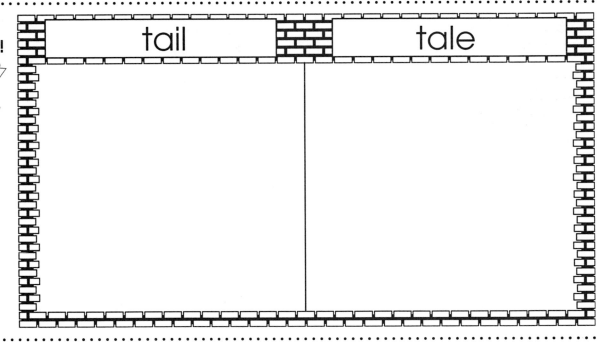

tail	tale

Tack it on!

Extend it!

Write a tale about " **The Famous Fish Tail**."

Dig in!

Use it!

Write each word in a sentence.

1. **tail**: _____

2. **tale**: _____

Set in concrete!

CEMENT

Say it! Write it!
Spell it!

Say it!	Write it!	Spell it! (Don't look!)
fair		
fare		

Nail it down!

Define it!

What does it mean? Look it up in the dictionary.

fair _____

_____

fare _____

_____

Create a blueprint!

Draw it!

fair	fare

Tack it on!

Extend it!

Pretend you are at the fair. The fare for each ride is 50 cents. If you go on two rides, how much would that cost? Five rides? Eight rides? Eleven rides? Show your work on a separate piece of paper.

Dig in!

Use it!

Write each word in a sentence.

1. **fair:**_____

2. **fare:**_____

SYNONYMS

earth/world

doctor/physician

couch/sofa

bucket/pail

bug/insect

detergent/soap

suitcase/luggage

truck/rig

chef/cook

present/gift

gas/petrol

What is a synonym?
A word that has the same or nearly the same meaning as another word.

earth • world

Set in concrete!

Say it! Write it!
Spell it!

Say it!	Write it!	Spell it! (Don't look!)
earth		
world		

Nail it down!

Define it!

What does it
mean? Look it up
in the dictionary.

earth/world

_____

_____

**Create
a blueprint!**

Draw it!

earth/world

Tack it on!

Extend it!

Locate the United States on a map or globe. What countries are on
the other side of the world? Name at least three.

Dig in!

Use it!

Write each word in a sentence.

1. **earth**: _____

2. **world**: _____

Name: _____

doctor • physician

Set in concrete!

Say it! Write it!
Spell it!

	Say it!	Write it!	Spell it! (Don't look!)
	doctor		
	physician		

Nail it down!

Define it!

What does it mean? Look it up in the dictionary.

doctor/physician

_____

_____

Create a blueprint!

Draw it!

doctor/physician

Tack it on!

Extend it!

Abbreviations are shortened forms of words.
What is the abbreviation for **doctor**?

Dig in!

(Use it!)

Write each word in a sentence.

1. **doctor**: _____

2. **physician**: _____

Name: _____

couch • sofa

Set in concrete!

Say it! Write it! Spell it!

	Say it!	Write it!	Spell it! (Don't look!)
	couch		
	sofa		

Nail it down!

Define it!

What does it mean? Look it up in the dictionary.

couch/sofa

_____

_____

Create a blueprint!

couch/sofa

Draw it!

Tack it on!

Extend it!

Draw your favorite place to sit and relax. What makes this place so special? Write a paragraph describing this place.

Dig in!

Use it!

Write each word in a sentence.

1. **couch:** _____

2. **sofa:** _____

 Reading FUNdamentals™ — Homonyms, Synonyms & Antonyms ©2009 Barker Creek Publishing, Inc. • www.barkercreek.com

Name: _____

bucket • pail

Reading FUNdamentals™ SYNONYMS

Set in concrete!

Say it! Write it! Spell it!

Say it!	Write it!	Spell it! (Don't look!)
bucket		
pail		

Nail it down!

Define it!

What does it mean? Look it up in the dictionary.

bucket/pail

_____

_____

Create a blueprint!

Draw it!

bucket/pail

Tack it on!

Extend it!

Illustrate this poem:
Jack and Jill went up the hill to fetch a pail of water.
Jack fell down and broke his crown, and Jill came tumbling after.

Dig in!

(Use it!)

Write each word in a sentence.

1. **bucket**:_____

2. **pail**:_____

bug • insect

Set in concrete! Say it! Write it! Spell it!	Say it!	Write it!	Spell it! (Don't look!)
	bug		
	insect		

Nail it down!

Define it!

What does it mean? Look it up in the dictionary.

bug/insect

_____

_____

Create a blueprint!

Draw it!

bug/insect

Tack it on!

Extend it!

Many bug names are compound words — two words put together to make one word. *(Example: lady+bug= ladybug)* On a separate piece of paper, make a list of other bug names that are compound words. Write at least six.

Dig in!

Use it!

Write each word in a sentence.

1. **bug**: _____

2. **insect**: _____

Name: _____

detergent • soap

Set in concrete!

Say it! Write it!
Spell it!

	Say it!	Write it!	Spell it! (Don't look!)
detergent			
soap			

Nail it down!

Define it!

What does it mean? Look it up in the dictionary.

detergent/soap

_____

_____

Create a blueprint!

Draw it!

detergent/soap

Tack it on!

Extend it!

Do you remember to wash your hands before you eat? To ensure that you wash thoroughly, while you are lathering, sing the *Happy Birthday* song. Keep washing until you sing the *entire* song. Now that's clean!

Dig in!

(Use it!)

Write each word in a sentence.

1. **detergent**: _____

2. **soap**: _____

suitcase • luggage

Set in concrete!

Say it! Write it! Spell it!

Say it!	Write it!	Spell it! (Don't look!)
suitcase		
luggage		

Nail it down!

Define it!

What does it mean? Look it up in the dictionary.

suitcase/luggage

_____

_____

Create a blueprint!

Draw it!

suitcase/luggage

Tack it on!

Extend it!

If you were going to take a trip to the moon and could take only 10 items, what would they be? List these on a separate piece of paper.

Dig in!

Use it!

Write each word in a sentence.

1. **suitcase**: _____

2. **luggage**: _____

Name: _____

truck • rig

Set in concrete!

Say it! Write it! Spell it!

Say it!	Write it!	Spell it! (Don't look!)
truck		
rig		

Nail it down!

Define it!

What does it mean? Look it up in the dictionary.

truck/rig

_____

_____

Create a blueprint!

Draw it!

truck/rig

Tack it on!

Extend it!

Draw a picture of a truck. Label its parts.

Dig in!

(Use it!)

Write each word in a sentence.

1. **truck**: _____

2. **rig**: _____

Name: _____

chef • cook

Set in concrete!

Say it! Write it!
Spell it!

Say it!	Write it!	Spell it! (Don't look!)
chef		
cook		

Nail it down!

Define it!

What does it
mean? Look it up
in the dictionary.

chef/cook

_____

_____

Create
a blueprint!

Draw it!

chef/cook

Tack it on!

Extend it!

Imagine that you are a chef at a very fancy restaurant. What
would definitely be on the menu? List at least five choices and
write a description for each as you would want them to appear
in your menu.

Dig in!

Use it!

Write each word in a sentence.

1. **chef**: _____

2. **cook**: _____

Name: _____

present • gift

Set in concrete!

Say it! Write it!
Spell it!

	Say it!	Write it!	Spell it! (Don't look!)
	present		
	gift		

Nail it down!

Define it!

What does it mean? Look it up in the dictionary.

present/gift

_____

_____

Create a blueprint!

Draw it!

present/gift

Tack it on!

Extend it!

Pretend you have wrapped a present in a box and no one knows what it is. Provide five very helpful clues to tell a partner. Can he/she guess what is in the box? You may have to give more clues.

Dig in!

(Use it!)

Write each word in a sentence.

1. **present**: _____

2. **gift**: _____

Name: _____

gas • fuel

Set in concrete!

Say it! Write it!
Spell it!

Say it!	Write it!	Spell it! (Don't look!)
gas		
fuel		

Nail it down!

Define it!

What does it mean? Look it up in the dictionary.

gas/fuel

_____

_____

Create a blueprint!

Draw it!

gas/fuel

Tack it on!

Extend it!

Assume your family's car holds 20 gallons of gas. How much money would it take to fill up the car's tank if the gas was $1.50 per gallon? $1.80 per gallon? $2.00 per gallon?

Dig in!

Use it!

Write each word in a sentence.

1. **gas**: _____

2. **fuel**: _____

ANTONYMS

What is an antonym?
A word that means the opposite of another word.

WORD LIST

infant/adult

empty/full

winter/summer

sunrise/sunset

miniature/gigantic

near/far

top/bottom

start/finish

east/west

frozen/melted

tall/short

Name: _____

infant • adult

Reading FUNdamentals™ ANTONYMS

Set in concrete!

Say it! Write it! Spell it!

Say it!	Write it!	Spell it! (Don't look!)
infant		
adult		

Nail it down!

Define it!

What does it mean? Look it up in the dictionary,

infant _____

_____

adult _____

_____

Create a blueprint!

Draw it!

infant	adult

Tack it on!

Extend it!

Using a magazine, cut out a picture of an infant.
Do the same for an adult. Compare each one.
How are they alike? How are they different?

Dig in!

Use it!

Write each word in a sentence.

1. **infant**: _____

2. **adult**: _____

Reading FUNdamentals™ — Homonyms, Synonyms & Antonyms ©2009 Barker Creek Publishing, Inc. • *www.barkercreek.com*

Name: _____

empty • full

Set in concrete!

Say it! Write it! Spell it!

Say it!	Write it!	Spell it! (Don't look!)
empty		
full		

Nail it down!

Define it!

What does it mean? Look it up in the dictionary,

empty _____

_____

full _____

_____

Create a blueprint!

Draw it!

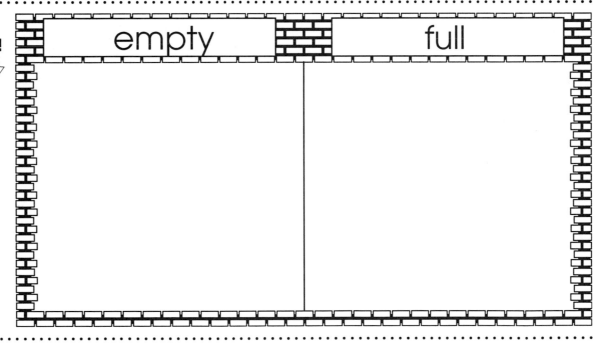

Tack it on!

Extend it!

Pour water into a container. Now empty it into a measuring cup to see how much the container holds.

Dig in!

Use it!

Write each word in a sentence.

1. **empty**: _____

2. **full**: _____

Set in concrete!

Say it! Write it!
Spell it!

Say it!	Write it!	Spell it! (Don't look!)
winter		
summer		

Nail it down!

Define it!

What does it
mean? Look it up
in the dictionary.

winter _____

_____

summer _____

_____

**Create
a blueprint!**

Draw it!

winter	summer

Tack it on!

Extend it!

List all of the winter and summer holidays.
Which holiday is your favorite? Why?

Dig in!

Use it!

Write each word in a sentence.

1. **winter**: _____

2. **summer**: _____

Name: _____

sunrise • sunset

Reading FUNdamentals™
ANTONYMS

Set in concrete!

Say it! Write it! Spell it!

	Say it!	Write it!	Spell it! (Don't look!)
	sunrise		
	sunset		

Nail it down!

Define it!

What does it mean? Look it up in the dictionary,

sunrise _____

_____

sunset _____

_____

Create a blueprint!

Draw it!

sunrise	sunset

Tack it on!

Extend it!

The sun rises in the _____ and sets in the _____.

Dig in!

Use it!

Write each word in a sentence.

1. **sunrise**: _____

2. **sunset**: _____

miniature • gigantic

Name: _____

Set in concrete!	Say it!	Write it!	Spell it! (Don't look!)
Say it! Write it! Spell it!	miniature		
	gigantic		

Nail it down!

Define it!

What does it mean? Look it up in the dictionary,

miniature _____

_____

gigantic _____

_____

Create a blueprint!

Draw it!

miniature	gigantic

Tack it on!

Extend it!

Draw a miniature elephant and a gigantic flea.
Write a creative story about them.

Dig in!

Use it!

Write each word in a sentence.

1. **miniature**: _____

2. **gigantic**: _____

 Reading FUNdamentals™ — Homonyms, Synonyms & Antonyms ©2009 Barker Creek Publishing, Inc. • *www.barkercreek.com*

Name: _____

near • far

Reading FUNdamentals™
ANTONYMS

Set in concrete!

Say it! Write it! Spell it!

Say it!	Write it!	Spell it! (Don't look!)
near		
far		

Nail it down!

Define it!

What does it mean? Look it up in the dictionary,

near _____

_____

far _____

_____

Create a blueprint!

Draw it!

near	far

Tack it on!

Extend it!

What relative lives nearest to you?
What relative lives the farthest away from you?

Dig in!

Use it!

Write each word in a sentence.

1. **near:** _____

2. **far:** _____

Name: _____

top • bottom

Set in concrete!

Say it! Write it! Spell it!

Say it!	Write it!	Spell it! (Don't look!)
top		
bottom		

Nail it down!

Define it!

What does it mean? Look it up in the dictionary,

top _____

_____

bottom _____

_____

Create a blueprint!

Draw it!

top	bottom

Tack it on!

Extend it!

Choose an object to describe in great detail from TOP to BOTTOM. Write this in paragraph form.

Dig in!

Use it!

Write each word in a sentence.

1. **top**: _____

2. **bottom**: _____

start • finish

Reading FUNdamentals™
ANTONYMS

Set in concrete!

Say it! Write it!
Spell it!

	Say it!	Write it!	Spell it! (Don't look!)
	start		
	finish		

Nail it down!

Define it!

What does it mean? Look it up in the dictionary,

start _____

_____

finish _____

_____

Create a blueprint!

Draw it!

start	finish

Tack it on!

Extend it!

How long does it take you to write the alphabet from START to FINISH (A-Z)? If it was under one minute, try writing it from FINISH to START (Z-A) this time. Which took longer?

Dig in!

Use it!

Write each word in a sentence.

1. **start**: _____

2. **finish**: _____

east • west

Set in concrete!

Say it! Write it!
Spell it!

	Say it!	Write it!	Spell it! (Don't look!)
	east		
	west		

Nail it down!

Define it!

What does it mean? Look it up in the dictionary,

east _____

_____

west _____

_____

Create a blueprint!

Draw it!

east	west

Tack it on!

Extend it!

Find your state on a map.
What is to the EAST of your state? What is to the WEST?

Dig in!

Use it!

Write each word in a sentence.

1. **east**: _____

2. **west**: _____

Name: _____

frozen • melted

Reading FUNdamentals™
ANTONYMS

Set in concrete!	**Say it!**	**Write it!**	**Spell it!** (Don't look!)
Say it! Write it! Spell it!	frozen		
	melted		

 Nail it down!

Define it!

What does it mean? Look it up in the dictionary,

frozen _____

_____

melted _____

_____

 Create a blueprint!

Draw it!

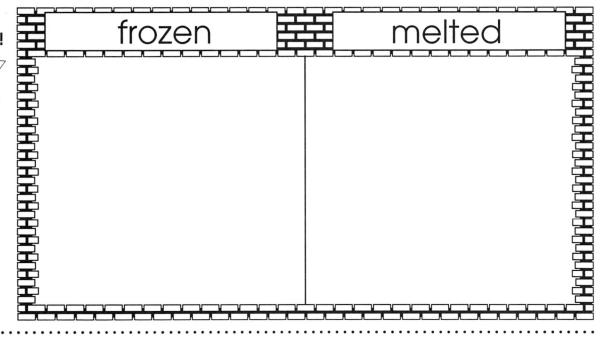

frozen	melted

 Tack it on!

Extend it!

Fold a piece of blue paper in half. On one side, paint a snowman. On the other side, paint a large sun and the snowman. What does this snowman look like? What happened?

 Dig in!

Use it!

Write each word in a sentence.

1. **frozen**: _____

2. **melted**: _____

Name: _____

tall • short

Set in concrete!

Say it! Write it! Spell it!

Say it!	Write it!	Spell it! (Don't look!)
tall		
short		

Nail it down!

Define it!

What does it mean? Look it up in the dictionary,

tall _____

_____

short _____

_____

Create a blueprint!

Draw it!

tall	short

Tack it on!

Extend it!

Illustrate a progression of an object going from TALL to SHORT. Use at least five different sizes for the same character.

Dig in!

Use it!

Write each word in a sentence.

1. **tall**: _____

2. **short**: _____

Reading FUNdamentals™ — Homonyms, Synonyms & Antonyms ©2009 Barker Creek Publishing, Inc. • www.barkercreek.com

Name: _____

HOMONYMS   Use the correct word in each sentence.
Write it in the blank.

1. A _____ contains seven days.
       week   weak

2. Make a _____ turn onto the next street.
       write   right

3. The _____ was not delivered yesterday. It was a holiday.
       male   mail

4. The rabbit's _____ was very soft and furry.
              tail   tale

5. Princess Lily was saved by the brave _____.
                              night   knight

SYNONYMS

Match the word to the left with its
synonym on the right.

1. pail   suitcase

2. luggage   physician

3. doctor   chef

4. rig   bucket

5. cook   truck

6. fuel   insect

7. bug   gas

ANTONYMS

What is the antonym for each word
listed below? Write it in the blank.

1. infant _____

2. frozen _____

3. gigantic _____

4. far   _____

5. start _____

6. melted _____

7. winter _____

Name: _____

●

Set in concrete!

Say it! Write it! Spell it!

Say it!	Write it!	Spell it! (Don't look!)

Nail it down!

Define it!

What does it mean? Look it up in the dictionary.

_____

_____

_____

Create a blueprint!

Draw it!

Tack it on!

Extend it!

_____

_____

_____

Dig in!

Use it!

Write each word in a sentence.

1. _____ _____

2. _____ _____

Name: _____

Set in concrete!

Say it! Write it! Spell it!

	Say it!	Write it!	Spell it! (Don't look!)

Nail it down!

Define it!

What does it mean? Look it up in the dictionary.

_____

_____

_____

_____

Create a blueprint!

Draw it!

Tack it on!

Extend it!

_____

_____

_____

Dig in!

(Use it!)

Write each word in a sentence.

1. _____ _____

2. _____ _____

Reading FUNdamentals™
ANTONYMS

Name: _____

Set in concrete!

Say it! Write it!
Spell it!

Say it!	Write it!	Spell it! (Don't look!)

Nail it down!

Define it!

What does it mean? Look it up in the dictionary,

_____ _____

_____

_____ _____

_____

Create a blueprint!

Draw it!

Tack it on!

Extend it!

_____

_____

_____

Dig in!

Use it!

Write each word in a sentence.

1. _____ _____

2. _____ _____

Reading FUNdamentals™ — Homonyms, Synonyms & Antonyms ©2009 Barker Creek Publishing, Inc. • www.barkercreek.com

flour

flower

bare

bear

male

mail

sale

sail

night

knight

hare

hair

HOMONYM PICTURES

week   weak   blue   blew

write   right   tail   tale

fair   fare

Reading FUNdamentals™ — Homonyms, Synonyms & Antonyms ©2009 Barker Creek Publishing, Inc. • www.barkercreek.com

earth / world

doctor / physician

couch / sofa

bucket / pail

bug / insect

detergent / soap

SYNONYM PICTURES

suitcase / luggage

truck / rig

chef / cook

present / gift

gas / fuel

Reading FUNdamentals™ — Homonyms, Synonyms & Antonyms ©2009 Barker Creek Publishing, Inc. • www.barkercreek.com

infant · adult · empty · full

winter · summer · sunrise · sunset

miniature · gigantic · near · far

ANTONYM PICTURES

top · bottom

start · finish

east · west

frozen · melted

tall · short

Reading FUNdamentals™ — Homonyms, Synonyms & Antonyms ©2009 Barker Creek Publishing, Inc. • *www.barkercreek.com*

LaVergne, TN USA
04 February 2010
172047LV00001B/52/P